The Five Mile Press

The Five Mile Press Pty Ltd
22 Summit Road
Noble Park Victoria 3174

First published 1998
This edition first published 1999

Printed in Singapore by KHL Printing Company

National Library of Australia
Cataloguing-in-Publication data
Barber, Shirley
Shirley Barber's count with me

ISBN 1 86463 053 1

1. Counting - Juvenile literature
I. Title II. Title: Count with me.
513.211

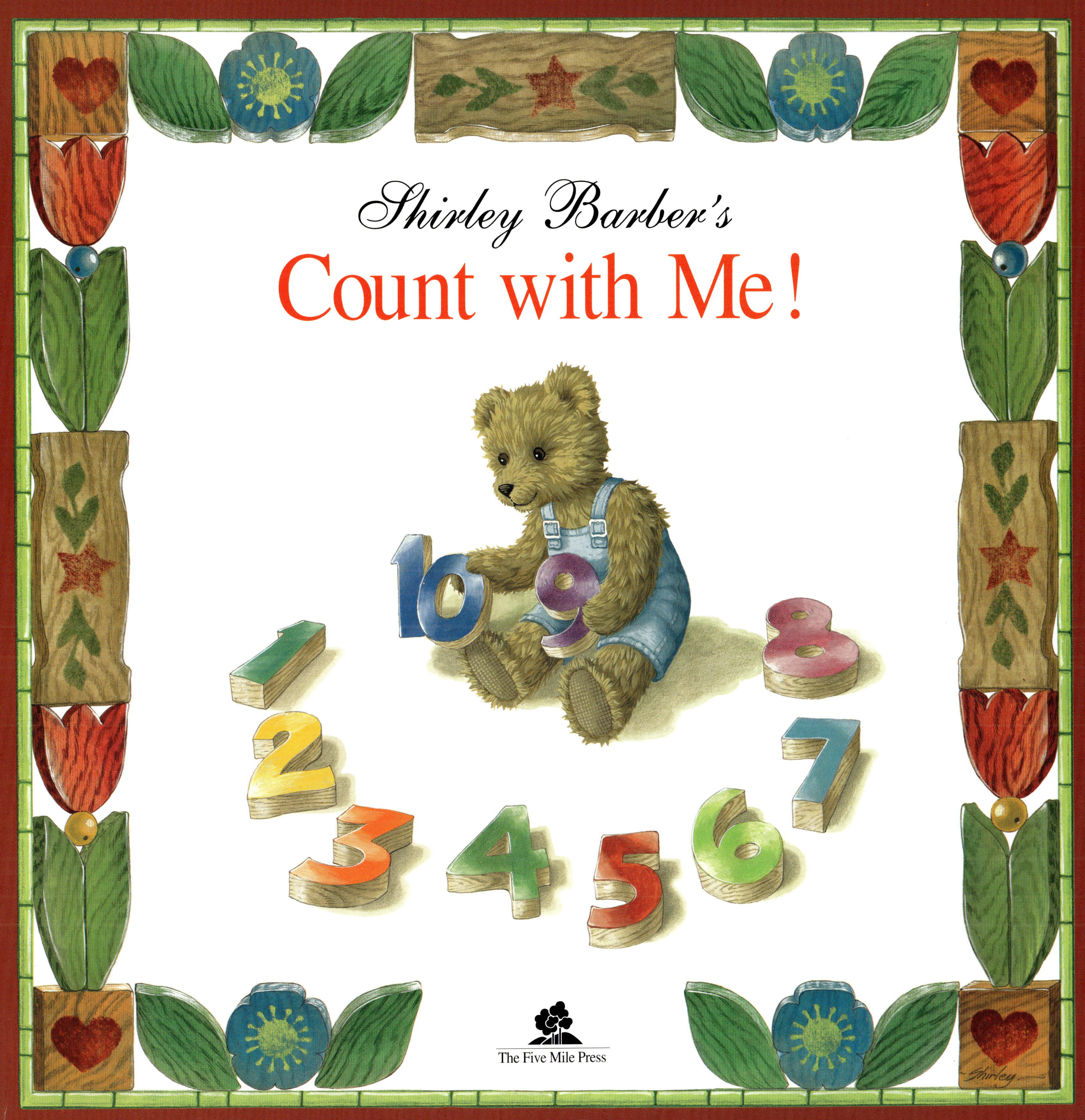
Shirley Barber's
Count with Me!
10
9
8
1
2
7
3
4
5
6
The Five Mile Press
Shirley

Come and count with me!

I can count 1 kitten riding his bike.
Can you see 1 snail?

Can you see 1 one of anything else?

Shirley

Now let's count to 2!

I can count 2 wooden dragons.
Can you see 2 teddies and 2 tigers?
Can you see 2 of anything else?

Count with me to 3!

I can count 3 bunnies and 3 bears.
Can you see 3 of anything else?

Shirley

Count with me to 4!

I can count 4 jewel boxes and 4 dolls.
Can you see 4 of anything else?

Shirley

Count with me to 5!

I can count 5 butterflies and 5 fairies.
Can you see 5 of anything else?

Count with me to 6!

I can count 6 bluebirds and 6 elves.
Can you see 6 of anything else?

Count with me to 7!

I can count 7 little bees and 7 cuddly pups.
Can you see 7 of anything else?

Shirley

Count with me to 8!

I can count 8 mice and 8 toy planes.
Can you see 8 of anything else?

Count with me to 9!

I can count 9 little houses and 9 playful kittens.
Can you see 9 of anything else?

Shirley

Now see if you can count right up to 10!

I can count 10 green frogs and 10 yellow ducklings.
Can you see 10 of anything else?

Shirley

10
9
8
7
6
5